TWISTED TOONS

Created by Rusty T & Lil' Bubb

For Twisted Toons Merchandise visit our Instagram or Facebook page for links.

I LIKE IT BETWEEN THE BEANS

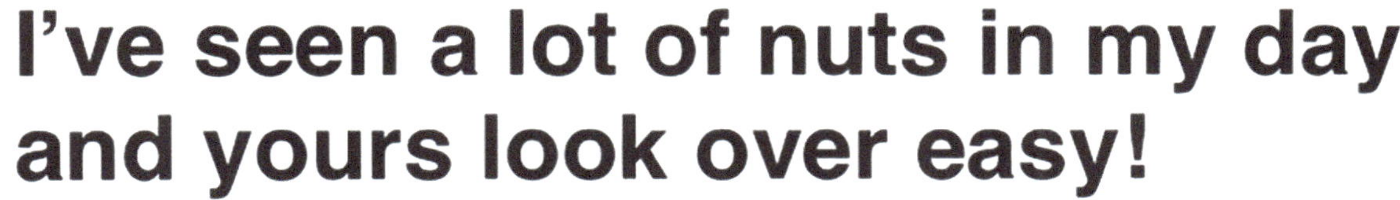
I've seen a lot of nuts in my day and yours look over easy!
Go away, I gotta do my magic.

I'm a front loader.
You look like one!

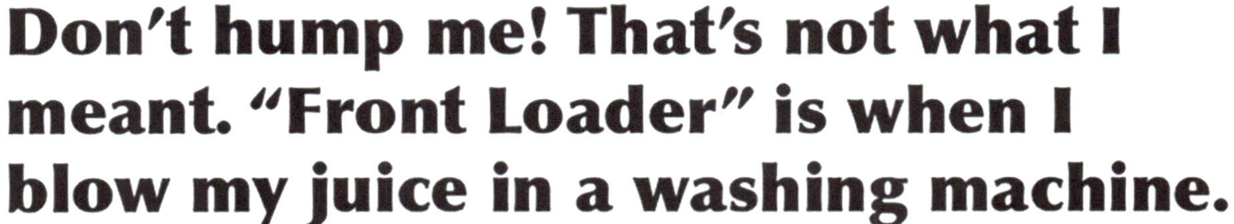
Don’t hump me! That’s not what I meant. “Front Loader” is when I blow my juice in a washing machine.

DRIVING MISS TWO NUTS

It looks like you've been licking a johnson.

ELECTRIC
BEEF
CURTAINS

What do you call that, Sam?
The NUTSTACHE!

Hey Ma'am!
Hey BONER!

RESTING DICKFACE

Remember that one time, Gus?
What time?
Yeah, me neither.
Shrooms? Anybody need shrooms?

I pierced my nipples, so I can walk more dogs.

I had a dream that my balls filled with helium and I flew above the city.

Double the chode, double my load!

Going pantless this year
It's the gift that keeps on giving.

I'm almost touching myself.

I see you and your balls are settled in for the evening.

That's what
I call banging
the berries.

We're making a pact, and that includes me.

What's the dumbest thing you've ever done while stoned?
Bought a book with a bunch of dumbass sayings in it.

Resting Dickface Gets A Promotion

Is that?
LOOK AWAY!
CLICK

Is it a sound, or is it Brown?

I'll turd on your niblets.

I'll pee in two of your holes!
Deal!

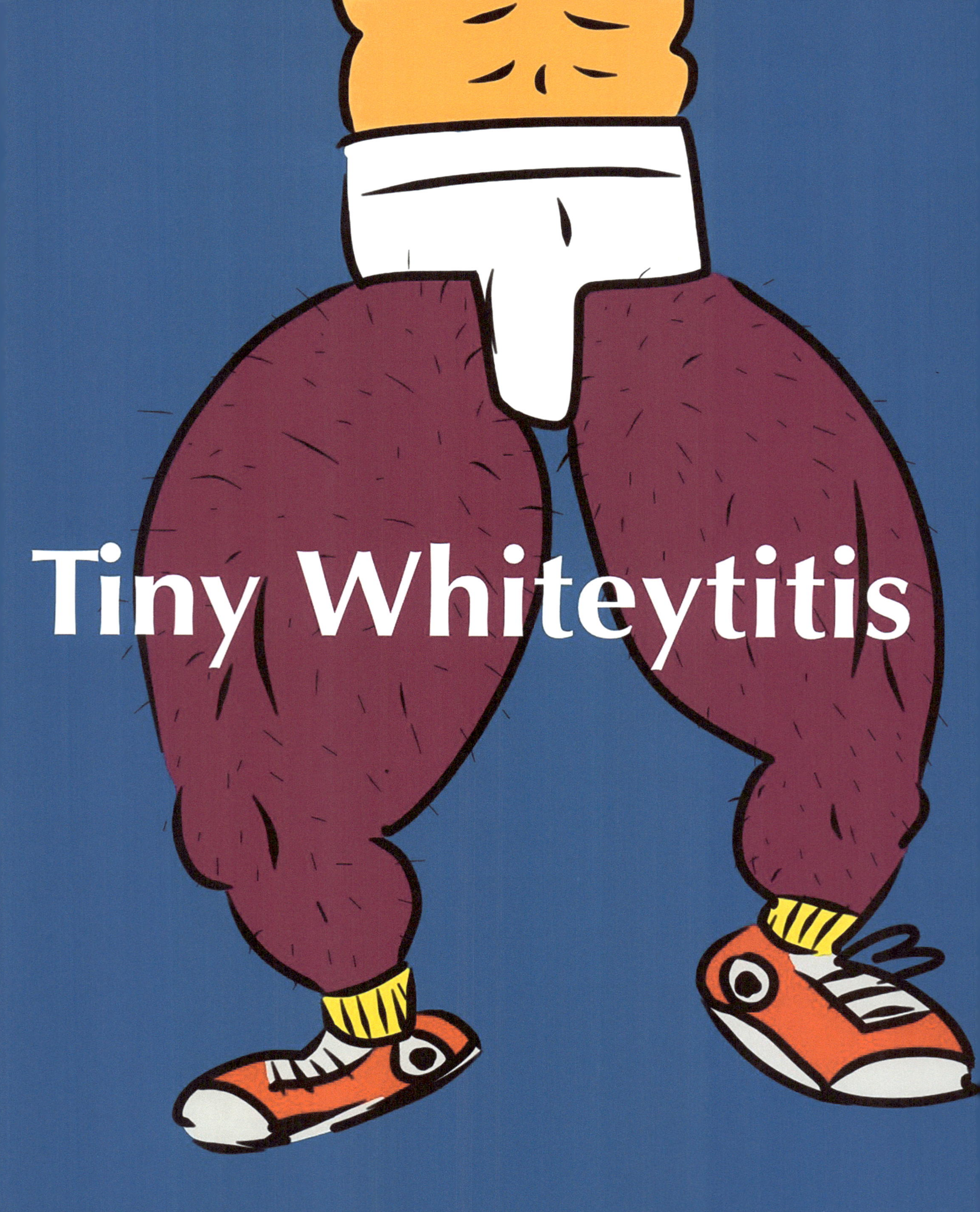
Tiny Whiteytitis

I LIKE IT ROUGH IN THE PUFF!
Lady, can I help you?

Are you house broken?
Are you circumcised?
RONNY

RESTING DICKFACE Goes on Vacation

MOONLIGHT.
CERVEZA.
SIDENUT.
¡Cubre tus frijoles!

I'm losing my mind!
Yeah and your neck.

Let there be no Weenus between us!
How big is YOUR Weenus?

Kiss my tits and smell my pits. Now get in the kitchen and cook me some grits.
Bite Me!

It was so embarrassing, I was chewing on this rubber toy for hours, turned out to be a vibrator.
Well, I've been humping stuffed animals for years. We all have our skeletons

It's not me, it's totally you.
You're an Asshole, Donny.

You're in your own world.
Me? No, I'm here.

Hey Ted! I see your kid is growing up fast, what grade is he in?
Pre-Scrotum.

LADY
OF
THE
LOAF

How's it hangin'?
Why do you ask?
No reason.

Release the sack!
Which one?

YOUR BREATH SMELLS LIKE FISH LIPS & ASSHOLES!

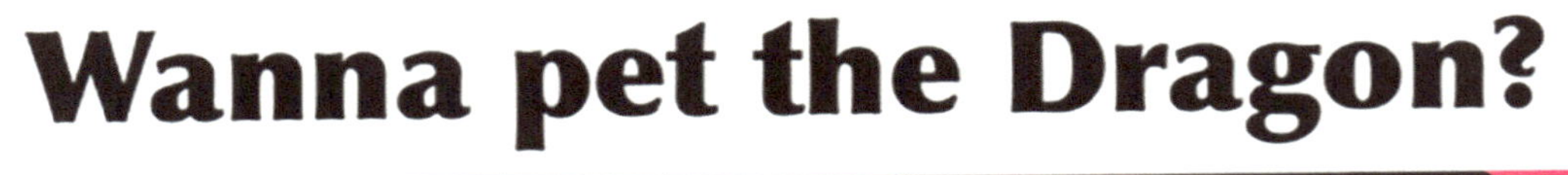
Wanna pet the Dragon?
I'm going to strangle that Sock Puppet!

See where that got you?

Serpent Spooge!

Long live the Queef!
You mean the Queen?
Yeah, her too!

Am I Pooping Soup?
Yeah, split pea and ham. The bathroom is over there.

You're Balls Deep!

NUTSCAPE

An amazing sunset. And my balls.

www.ingramcontent.com/pod-product-compliance
Lightning Source LLC
Chambersburg PA
CBHW042120030726
47599CB00002B/287
9780578472942